LIGHTNING BOLT BOOKS™

# Can You Tell a Stegosaurus from an Ankylosaurus?

Buffy Silverman

Lerner Publications Company
Minneapolis

To Ann,
my StegoSister
—B.S.

Lerner Publications Company
A division of Lerner Publishing Group, Inc.
241 First Avenue North
Minneapolis, MN 55401 U.S.A.

Website address: www.lernerbooks.com

Library of Congress Cataloging-in-Publication Data

Silverman, Buffy.
    Can you tell a stegosaurus from an ankylosaurus? / by Buffy Silverman.
        p.    cm. — (Lightning bolt books™—Dinosaur look-alikes)
    Includes index.
    ISBN 978-1-4677-1359-7 (lib. bdg. : alk. paper)
    ISBN 978-1-4677-1757-1 (eBook)
    1. Stegosaurus—Juvenile literature.  2. Ankylosaurus—Juvenile literature.  3. Dinosaurs—Juvenile literature.  I. Title.
    QE862.O65S563  2014
    567.915—dc23                                                    2013001103

Manufactured in the United States of America
1 — BP — 7/15/13

# Table of Contents

# Body Armor

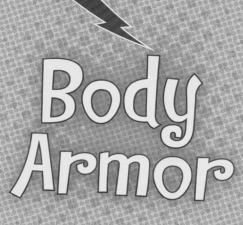

Imagine living when dinosaurs roamed Earth. Ferns grew as tall as trees. Some dinosaurs chewed these tall ferns. Other dinosaurs hunted for food.

How did plant eaters stay safe? Many had thick armor. Their bodies were covered with spikes and plates.

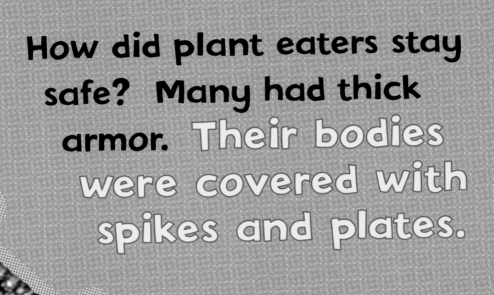

The body of this Ankylosaurus is covered in armor.

Dinosaurs with body armor belonged to a group called Thyreophora. Thyreophora means "shield bearers."

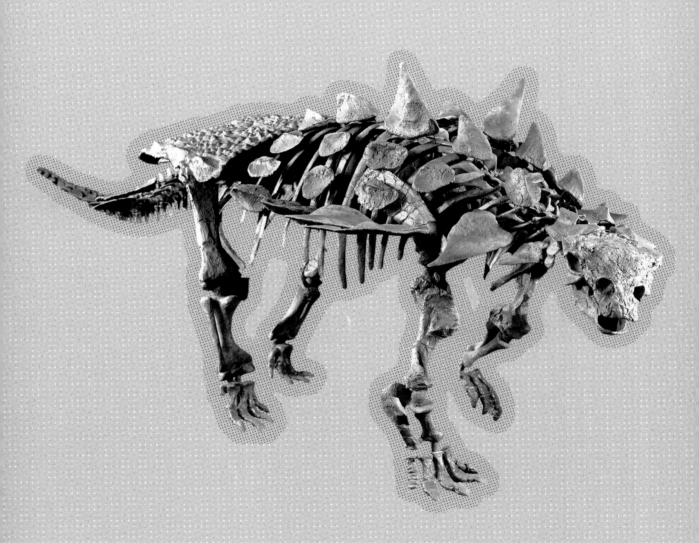

Stegosaurus and Ankylosaurus were Thyreophora. Their armor kept them safe.

An African elephant is the largest living land animal. Stegosaurus (above) and Ankylosaurus each grew about as long as an elephant.

Small plates covered
Ankylosaurus's head and jaw.
Horns stuck out above and
below its eyes.

This Ankylosaurus skull
shows the horns that
stuck out around its eyes.

Small round bones covered Stegosaurus's throat. They protected its neck.

Hundreds of plates and knobs covered Ankylosaurus's back. Some were as small as a penny. Others were bigger than a dinner plate.

Ankylosaurus armor stopped predators' claws and teeth. Scientists think it was as strong as a bulletproof vest!

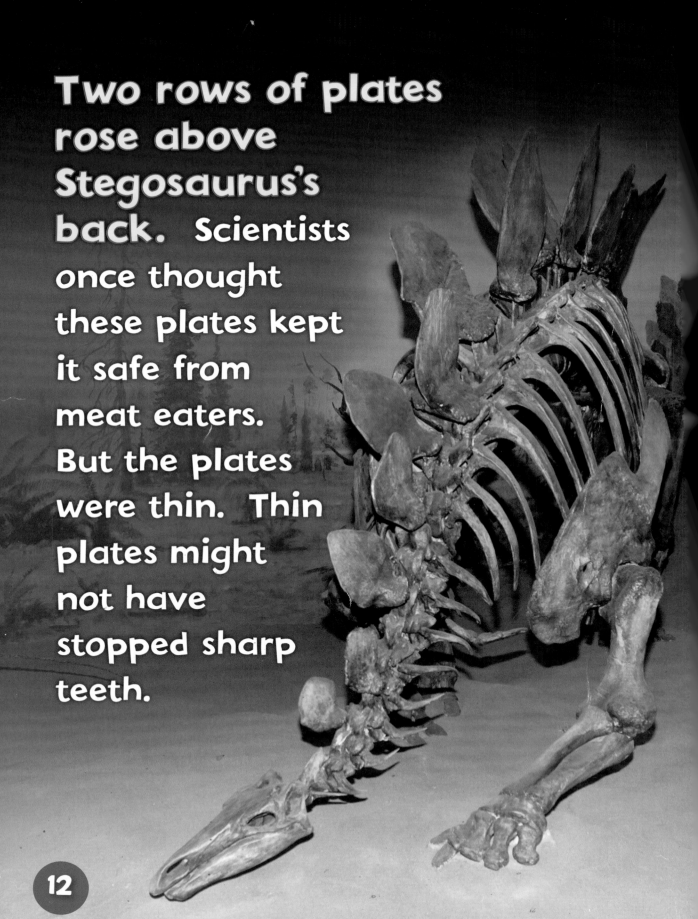

Two rows of plates rose above Stegosaurus's back. Scientists once thought these plates kept it safe from meat eaters. But the plates were thin. Thin plates might not have stopped sharp teeth.

The plates made Stegosaurus look bigger than it was. That might have scared predators. The plates might have helped Stegosaurus attract mates too.

Plates could also have helped Stegosaurus warm up and cool down.

# Tails: Spikes or Clubs?

Stegosaurus and Ankylosaurus had armor on their tails. They used the tails as weapons.

Several bones formed
Ankylosaurus's strong tail.
The tail ended in a round
club.  Ankylosaurus swung it
at enemies.

Four sharp spikes grew from Stegosaurus's tail. The creature whipped its tail from side to side.

This tail's sharp spikes stopped predators.

Ankylosaurus's swinging tail
could crush enemy bones.
The club struck with the force
of a bowling ball.

Ankylosaurus rivals
might have fought
with their tails when
looking for mates.

Stegosaurus sometimes broke a tail spike. The spikes could break off when Stegosaurus hit its enemies. Dinosaur fossils have been found with spike-sized holes.

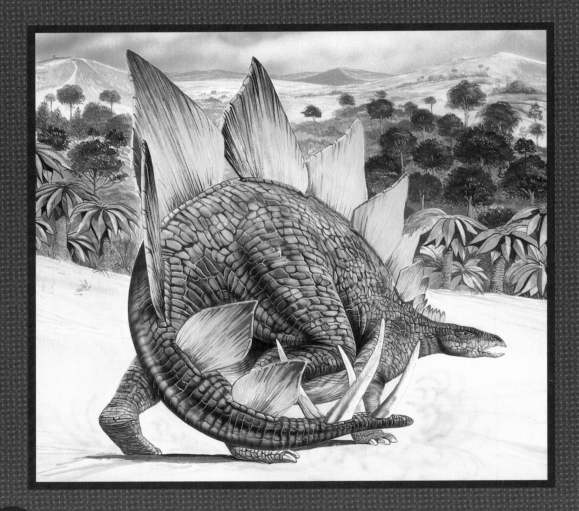

# Two Legs or Four?

Stegosaurus probably stood on all four feet when it swung its heavy tail. It needed good balance. Its front legs were shorter than its back legs. But they were strong.

Scientists study tracks to learn how dinosaurs moved. Some Stegosaurus tracks show that it might have sometimes walked on two feet.

Dinosaurs left tracks when they walked. Some tracks turned to fossils.

Ankylosaurus had short front legs too. It walked on four feet.

When you run, your footprints are far apart. Ankylosaurus tracks show that it might have jogged.

# Finding Food

Ankylosaurus found plants growing close to the ground. It stripped off their leaves.

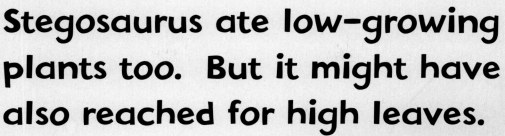

Stegosaurus ate low-growing plants too. But it might have also reached for high leaves. Some scientists think it stood on its back legs.

Stegosaurus's tail probably helped it balance.

23

Ankylosaurus had a wide head. It grabbed leaves with its beak.

Ankylosaurus cut plants with its small, leaf-shaped teeth.

Ankylosaurus did not chew its food. It swallowed whole leaves. The leaves sat inside Ankylosaurus for a long time. Ankylosaurus might have made a lot of gas!

Stegosaurus's head was tiny, long, and narrow. It had a beak and leaf-shaped teeth.

Stegosaurus brains were about the size of a lime!

Stegosaurus could grind up leaves. It stuffed leaves in its cheeks while it chewed. It probably swallowed small stones to help mash up its food.

# Dino Diagrams

## Can you tell these dinosaurs apart?

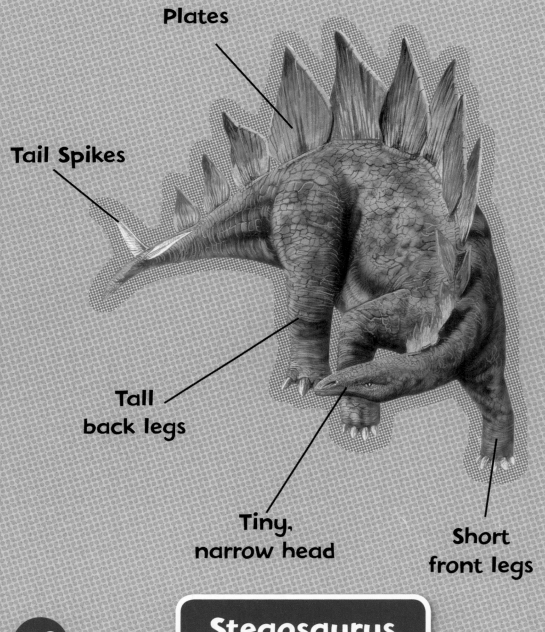

Plates

Tail Spikes

Tall back legs

Tiny, narrow head

Short front legs

**Stegosaurus**

# Ankylosaurus

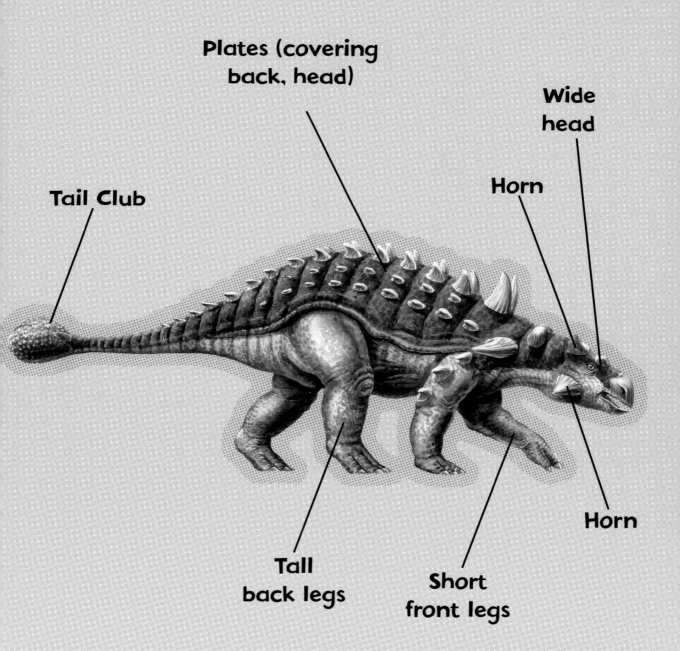

Plates (covering back, head)

Wide head

Horn

Tail Club

Tall back legs

Short front legs

Horn

# Glossary

**armor:** a tough, bony covering

**bearer:** holder

**fossil:** the remains of a living thing from a long time ago

**horn:** a hard structure that projects from the head of an animal

**plate:** a smooth, flat structure. Plates can cover the outside of an animal.

**predator:** an animal that hunts another animal

**shield:** something that protects

**spike:** a long, sharp, pointed object

**Thyreophora:** a group of plant-eating dinosaurs with armor

**track:** footprint

**weapon:** a part or organ that an animal uses in an attack or a defense

# Further Reading

Brecke, Nicole, and Patricia M. Stockland. *Dinosaurs and Other Prehistoric Creatures You Can Draw.* Minneapolis: Millbrook Press, 2010.

Galvin, Laura Gates. *Ankylosaurus Fights Back.* Smithsonian's Prehistoric Pals series. Norwalk, CT: Soundprints, 2007.

Landau, Elaine. *Stegosaurus.* True Books: Dinosaurs series. Danbury, CT: Children's Press, 2007.

Lessem, Don. *National Geographic Kids Ultimate Dinopedia: The Most Complete Dinosaur Reference Ever.* Washington, DC: National Geographic, 2010.

National Geographic Kids Creature Features— *Ankylosaurus magniventris*
http://kids.nationalgeographic.com/kids/animals/creaturefeature/ankylosaurus-magniventris

Vertebrate Paleo Team Field Work
http://paleobiology.si.edu/dinosaurs/collection/labs/fossiLab/index.html

Virtual Dinosaur Dig
http://paleobiology.si.edu/dinosaurs/interactives/dig/main.html

# Index

# Photo Acknowledgments

The images in this book are used with the permission of: © Jean-Michel Girard/Shutterstock.com, p. 1 (top); © Linda Bucklin/Shutterstock.com, pp. 1 (bottom), 14 (left); © Corey A. Ford/Dreamstime.com, p. 2; © Kayte Deioma/Zuma Press/Alamy, pp. 4, 26; © Christian Martinez Kempin/E+/Getty Images, p. 5; © Francois Gohier/Science Source, pp. 6, 10; © Albert T. Copley/Visuals Unlimited/CORBIS, p. 7; © WitmerLab at Ohio University, p. 8; © Ken Lucas/Visuals Unlimited/CORBIS, p. 9; © MasPix/Alamy, p. 11; Designs Pics/Peter Langer/Newscom, p. 12; © Roger Harris/Science Source, p. 13; © De Agnostini Picture Library/Getty Images, pp. 14 (right), 15, 18, 21, 23, 28; © National Geographic Society/CORBIS, p. 16; © Leonello Calvetti/Dreamstime.com, p. 17; © Leonello Calvetti/Shutterstock.com, p. 19; © David Mercado/Reuters/CORBIS, p. 20; © Christian Jegou/Science Source, p. 22; © The Natural History Museum/The Image Works, pp. 24, 27, 29; © Roger Harris/Science Source, p. 25; © Vaclav Volrab/Dreamstime.com, p. 30.

Front cover: © Leonello Calvetti/Dreamstime.com (top); © Vaclav Volrab/Dreamstime.com (bottom).

Main body text set in Johann Light 30/36.